Copyright © 1976 by Incentive Publications, Inc. All rights reserved. No part of this publication may be reproduced, stored in a retrieval system, or transmitted, in any form or by any means, electronic, mechanical, photocopying, recording, or otherwise, without prior written permission of Incentive Publications.

ISBN 0-913916-22-6
Library of Congress Catalog Card Number 76-3061

Printed in Nashville, Tennessee
by Incentive Publications
Box 12522
Nashville, Tennessee 37212

TABLE OF CONTENTS

Abbreviated Treasures....(abbreviations)	6
Action Spellers....(verbs)	8
Alphabet Adventure....(word recall)	10
Animal Answers....(animal names)	12
Blender's Bad....(blends)	14
Briefly Stated....(abbreviations)	16
Calendar Clues....(days of the week and dates)	18
Calling All Consonants....(consonants)	20
Carpenter's Craze....(auditory context clues)	22
Category Capers....(categorization)	24
Chain Gang....(reinforcement drill)	26
Classy Contractions....(contractions)	28
Comic Contest....(transferal)	30
Compound Corner....(compound words)	32
Computer Cranny....(word construction)	34
Cook's Choice....(food names)	36
Daring Darts....(drill)	38
Dazzling Detectives....(creative recall)	40
Double Duty....(word extension)	42
Freaky Fortunes....(present and past tense)	44
Funny Feelings....(emotions)	46
Great Guessers....(picture clues)	48
Holiday Hunt....(holidays)	50
Homonym House....(homonyms)	52
Hopscotch Holdup....(nouns)	54
Look and Spell....(picture identification)	56
Map Makers....(functional usage)	58

Math Monster....(math vocabulary)	60
Mountain Climbers....(enrichment)	62
Park and Lock....(reinforcement)	64
Perfect Ending....(word endings)	66
Pick Pockets....(vowels)	68
Picture Play...(environmental vocabulary)	70
Plural Picnic....(plurals)	72
Puzzling Pieces....(word meanings)	74
Rain Drop Delight....(reinforcement)	76
Right or Wrong....(decision making)	78
Role Review....(occupations)	80
Root Relay....(root words)	82
Shake and Make....(word construction)	84
Sight Seeing....(situational vocabulary)	86
Silent Scoop....(silent letters)	88
Speech Splash....(parts of speech)	90
Spelling Scramble....(scrambled words)	92
Spinner Spree....(enrichment)	94
Star Gazers....(rhyming words)	96
Surprise Store....(consumer vocabulary)	98
T for Three....(vocabulary extension)	100
Television Talent....(enrichment)	102
Travel Tips....(personal recall)	104
Variety Victory....(antonyms, homonyms, and synonyms)	106
Vowel Voyage....(vowels)	108
Window Shopping....(functional vocabulary)	110

Oh, no! It's spelling time again! In too many elementary classrooms today this expresses the attitudes of both teachers and students. Weekly lists, workbooks, and/or highly structured programs have taken all the fun out of teaching and learning spelling skills.

No one is advocating a return to the days of the blue back speller and the Friday spelldown. There is, however, something to be said for the motivation afforded by an overtly active approach to the development of a desire for excellence in spelling. That's what this book is all about! It is a collection of activities, gimmicks, and games galore for making learning mean lots more! Its purpose is to help teachers make spelling come alive in their own classrooms, and to encourage boys and girls to become personally involved in spontaneous learning experiences.

The activities have been planned to meet needs and interests of students with differing abilities and interests, and to be implemented in a variety of classroom settings. Their use is not limited to open space, traditional, or any other organizational arrangement. Many of them are adaptable for use with the entire class; others are designed for a small group, i.e. for two, three, or four students; and some may be enjoyed by an individual student.

Game boards, posters, and gimmicks have been designed to be easily produced, stored, and implemented. The materials necessary for their construction have been limited to those readily available in most classrooms and call for no special artistic ability. In many instances, students themselves will want to become involved in the selection and preparation of activities most appropriate for use in their own classrooms.

We hope that this collection will bring a spark of

to teachers and students who use it.

Imogene Forte
Mary Ann Pangle

ABBREVIATED TREASURES

Preparation Directions:

1. Prepare three lists of words to abbreviate. Days of the week, months of the year, professions, and titles are classifications that may be used.

2. Reproduce copies of the treasure hunt map on the following page and print in specific directions to make it "fit" your classroom.

3. Roll the word lists up and tie with brightly colored yarn or ribbon.

4. Cover four cigar or shoe boxes with contact or gift wrap paper to resemble treasure chests. Place word lists in each treasure chest and print the corresponding abbreviations on the bottom of each box to be used as an answer key.

Player Directions:

1. This is a "free time" activity and may be used by any number of students.

2. The students are to follow the map to the first place designated, take out a rolled-up sheet, write the correctly spelled abbreviation beside each word, and check their work by using the answer key on the bottom of the box. They then move to the next two stations and follow the same procedure.

3. The fourth treasure chest should be entitled "Last Stop for Treasure Hunters", and should afford a candy treat or other small surprise.

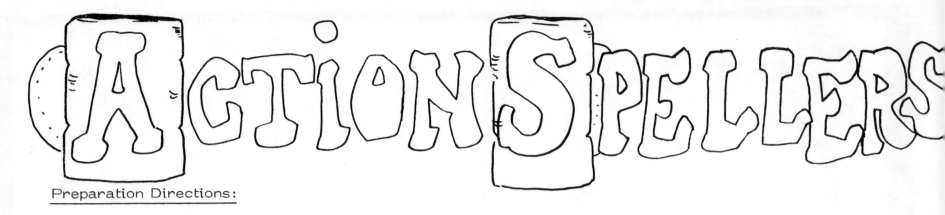

Action Spellers

Preparation Directions:

1. Cover a coffee can with brightly colored contact paper.

2. Print the following words on squares of cardboard.

run	write
hop	sleep
skip	wink
jump	wave
laugh	clap
smile	drink
eat	swim

3. Place the cards in the covered coffee can.

Player Directions:

1. This game is for two or three players.

2. One player draws a card, reads the word silently, and pantomimes the word.

3. The first player to guess and spell the word correctly gets to keep the card.

4. The game continues until all cards have been pantomimed.

5. The player with the most cards wins the game.

Alphabet Adventure

Preparation Directions:

1. Provide a copy of the maze, a pencil, and crayons for each player.

Player Directions:

1. This game is for any number of players.

2. Using a pencil, the first player enters the maze but must stop when a letter of the alphabet appears.

3. The player spells a word that begins with that letter and the word must contain at least five letters.

4. The game continues until one player completes the maze and wins the game.

5. The players may wish to color the maze or create a maze of their own for classmates to complete.

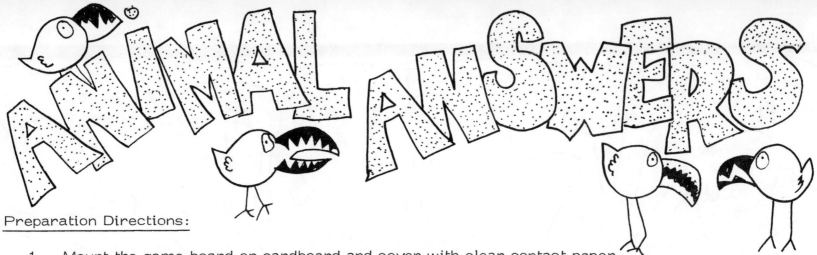

ANIMAL ANSWERS

Preparation Directions:

1. Mount the game board on cardboard and cover with clear contact paper.

2. Provide markers for each player.

3. Print "one" on ten small squares of tagboard; print "two" on five small squares; print "three" on three small squares; print "go back one space" on two small squares; print "move ahead one space" on four small squares.

Player Directions:

1. This game is for two, three, or four players.

2. Each player places a marker on "Zoo Entrance".

3. The cards are shuffled and placed face down.

4. The first player draws a card, moves the correct number of spaces, and must correctly spell the name of the animal in the picture.

5. If the animal is not spelled correctly, the player must go back to the last starting position.

6. The game continues until the first player reaches "Zoo Exit" and wins the game.

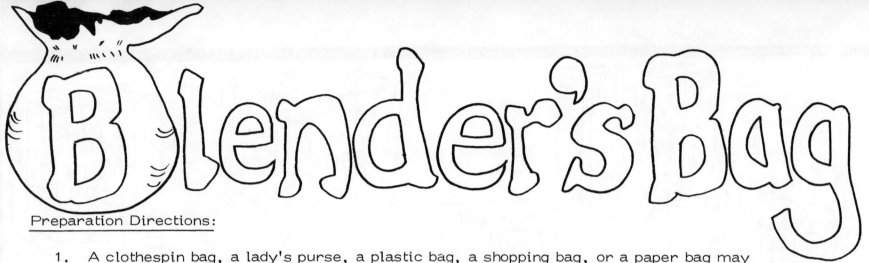

Blender's Bag

Preparation Directions:

1. A clothespin bag, a lady's purse, a plastic bag, a shopping bag, or a paper bag may be used for this game.

2. Write different blends on index cards.

3. Place the blend cards in the bag.

Player Directions:

1. This game is for any number of players.

2. Each player needs paper and a pencil.

3. Place the blend bag in the center of the players.

4. One player draws a blend card and holds it up for all the players to see.

5. At a given signal, the players write words that contain the blend.

6. The game continues until all the blend cards have been drawn.

7. The player who has the most correctly spelled words wins the game.

Preparation Directions:

1. Reproduce one copy of the outline map on the following page for each of the players.

2. Prepare lists of the names of the fifty states on the map.

3. Provide pencils and an answer key.

Player Directions:

1. This activity is for any number of players.

2. Distribute outline map, lists, and pencils.

3. The game begins at a given signal. Players are to identify the states on the map and write the abbreviation of the state's name on the correct space. The lists of full names of the states may be used for reference if needed.

4. The first player to label the entire map with correctly spelled abbreviations wins the game.

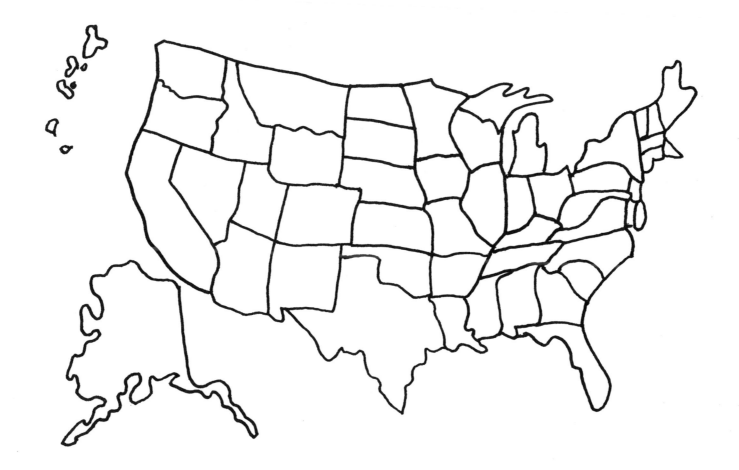

CALENDAR CLUES

Preparation Directions:

1. Use tagboard and several colors of felt tip markers to make a calendar for one month.

2. Decorate the calendar by drawing appropriate small pictures to make a border or by using pictures cut from magazines or old textbooks.

3. Provide a small cube.

Player Directions:

1. This game is for two or four players.

2. The first player tosses the cube on the calendar. The player must spell the day of the week and/or the date number on which the cube lands.

3. If the player spells the day of the week correctly, one point is given. If the date number is spelled correctly, two points are received.

4. The game continues until one player receives fifteen points and wins the game.

CALENDAR CLUES

S	M	T	W	T	F	S
		1	2	3	4	5
6	7	8	9	10	11	12
13	14	15	16	17	18	19
20	21	22	23	24	25	26
27	28	29	30			

Calling All Consonants

Preparation Directions:

1. Print one consonant on each of twenty-one index cards.

2. Draw pictures on twenty-one index cards to correspond with the beginning sound on each of the twenty-one printed cards.

3. Provide writing paper and pencils.

Player Directions:

1. This game is for four or six players.

2. The cards are shuffled and dealt to the players.

3. The players check for "pairs" in the cards. A "pair" is one consonant card and a picture card that has the same beginning consonant sound. The "pairs" are placed on the table.

4. The first player draws a card from another player. If a matching card is drawn, the player places the "pair" on the table.

5. The game continues until all the cards have been drawn.

6. The players use writing paper to write the names of the pictures in the "pairs".

7. The player with the most "pairs" spelled correctly wins the game.

Preparation Directions:

Tape the following directions:

"Today we are going to pretend to be carpenters. Take a sheet of drawing paper and a sheet of writing paper. You will need a pencil and crayons. Listen carefully to the directions.

"On the drawing paper draw the outline of a house. For the title write the word "house" on the writing paper. Add the roof to your house and write the word "roof". Your house needs a chimney. Try to spell "chimney" correctly. The house needs a door. Add it and spell the word "door". Did you add a door knob? Remember that word has a silent letter, so be careful when spelling it. How many windows will your house need? When you have drawn the windows, write the word "windows". Make shutters for your windows and write the word. Is your house made from wood, stone, or brick? Add that to the house and write either the word "wood", "stone", or "brick". Now that the house is complete, you need to make a sidewalk. Write the word "sidewalk". Plant grass around your house and write the word "grass". Add flowers and shrubs. Write the words "flowers" and "shrubs".

"Now let us check the spelling of the words you have written. If you miss a word, please correct it.

1. house
2. roof
3. chimney
4. door
5. door knob
6. windows
7. shutters
8. wood – stone – brick
9. sidewalk
10. grass
11. flowers – shrubs

"Color your picture to make it more attractive. When you finish, mount your picture on the bulletin board to share with your classmates."

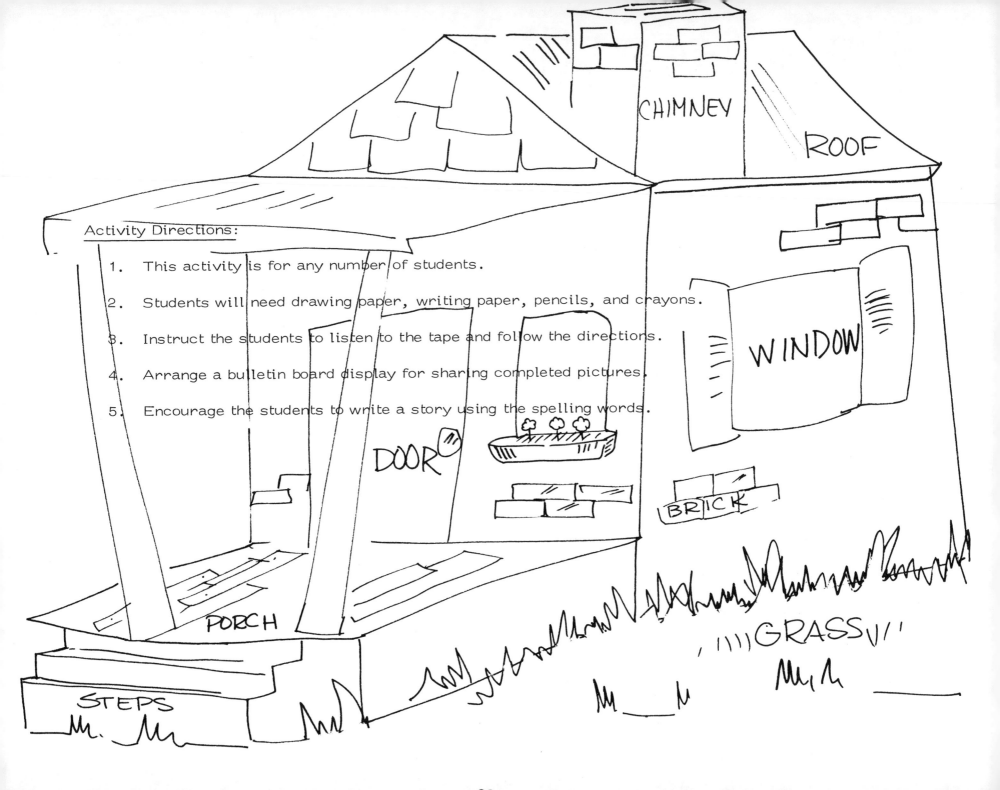

Activity Directions:

1. This activity is for any number of students.
2. Students will need drawing paper, writing paper, pencils, and crayons.
3. Instruct the students to listen to the tape and follow the directions.
4. Arrange a bulletin board display for sharing completed pictures.
5. Encourage the students to write a story using the spelling words.

Preparation Directions:

1. Print words in the following categories on index cards:

    flowers   clothing
    foods   months
    sports   states
                             household articles

Other categories may be added.

2. Place word categories in envelopes.

3. Label the envelopes according to the category.

Player Directions:

1. This game is for any number of players.

2. One player is selected to be the leader.

3. The players are divided into two teams.

4. Players take turns selecting categories.

5. The leader draws a card from that category and pronounces the word.

6. One point is given to that team for each correctly spelled word.

7. The game continues until one team scores fifteen points and wins the game.

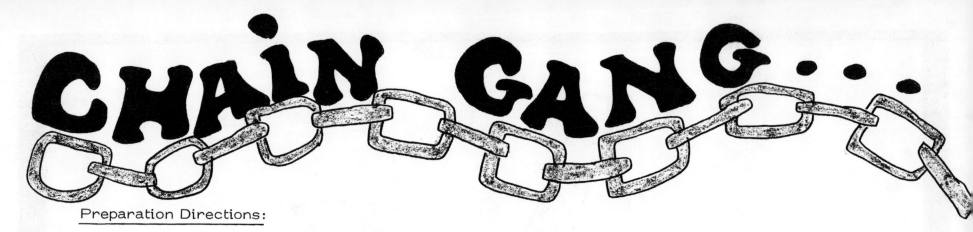

Preparation Directions:

1. Cut fifty 1" x 3" strips from different colors of construction paper.

2. Provide glue and pencils.

3. Provide a spelling word list containing fifty words. The words can be from the spelling book, unit words, or a variety of words.

Player Directions:

1. This game is for the entire class.

2. The class is divided into two equal groups.

3. Place the strips of construction paper, glue, and pencils on a table.

4. The teacher pronounces a word.

5. One member from each team walks to the table, writes the word on a strip of paper, and hands the strips to the teacher. The teacher checks the spelling. If the word is spelled correctly, the player glues the strip together to form one link of a chain.

6. The game continues until all the words are used, with the players adding one link to their team's chain as a word is spelled correctly.

7. The team with the longest chain wins the game.

CLASSY CONTRACTIONS

Preparation Directions:

1. Write words from which contractions can be made on 2" x 3" strips of paper.

   Example: is not   should not   I am

2. Provide twelve quart-size soft drink bottles.

3. Tape the words on the bottles.

4. Provide an embroidery hoop.

Player Directions:

1. This game is for two players.

2. Place the bottles in a triangular shape as bowling pins are arranged.

3. The first player tosses the hoop and tries to "ring" a bottle.

4. The player pronounces the words on the bottle and spells the contraction for the words. If the contraction is correctly spelled, the player receives one point.

5. The game continues until all the contractions are spelled correctly.

6. The player who has the most points wins the game.

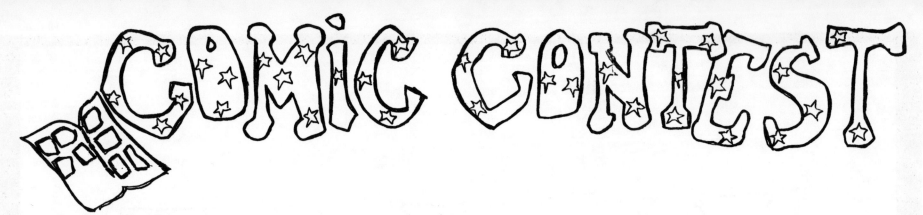

Preparation Directions:

1. Paste comic strips from the newspaper on the inside of letter-size manila folders.

2. Decorate the front of the folders.

3. Write the directions for the game on the back of the folders.

Player Directions:

1. This game is for two players.

2. Each player selects a folder and reads the comics.

3. The first player chooses a word from any of the comics and asks the second player to spell it.

4. The player receives one point if the word is spelled correctly.

5. The game continues until one player receives fifteen points and wins the game.

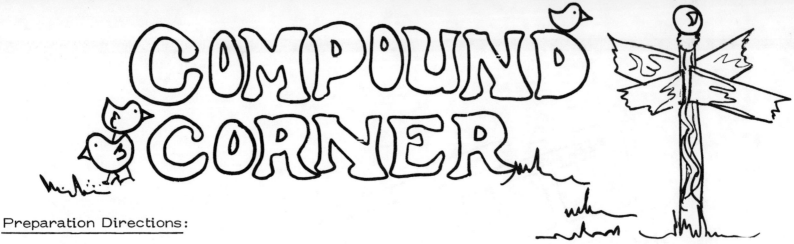

COMPOUND CORNER

Preparation Directions:

1. Write words that can be made into compound words on forty strips of poster board.

2. Prepare the game board.

3. Cut along the broken lines on the game board to create pockets to hold the word cards.

4. Paste paper on the underside of the game board to reinforce the pockets.

Player Directions:

1. This game is for two players.

2. Place the word cards face down in the pockets on the game board.

3. The first player selects two cards.

4. If the two cards form a compound word, the player spells that word and keeps the card.

5. If the cards do not form a compound word, the player places the cards back in the pockets on the game board.

6. The game continues until all of the cards have been used to form compound words.

7. The player with the most compound words wins the game.

Preparation Directions:

1. Make a computer by pasting twenty-one library pockets on a piece of poster board.

2. Print a consonant on each library pocket.

3. Cut a circle three inches in diameter from tagboard. Print the vowels on the circle and attach the circle to the poster board.

4. Provide 3" x 5" index cards and pencils.

Player Directions:

1. This game is for two, three, or four players.

2. The first player selects a consonant on the computer panel and turns the vowel button.

3. Using the index cards, all the players write words containing the consonant and vowel from the computer, plus adding another consonant.

    Example: Computer Panel   +   Vowel Button   +   Another Consonant   =

                     b   +   i   +   g   =   big

4. The index cards are placed in the library pockets.

5. The game continues until one player has a total of fifty words on all of the index cards.

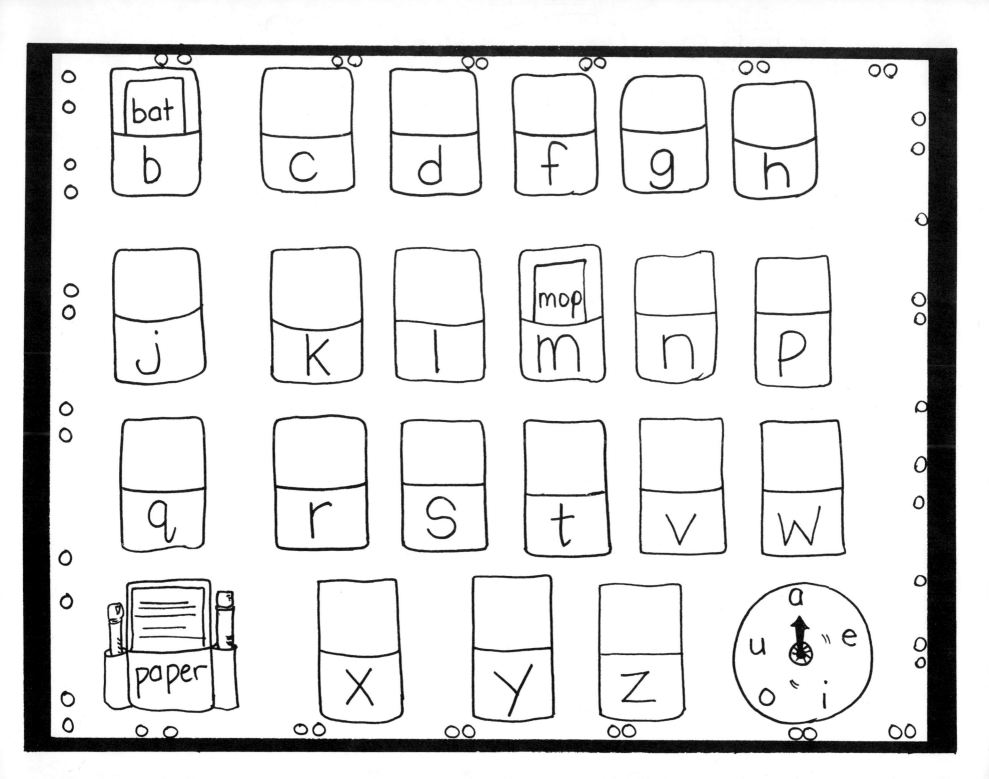

COOK'S CHOICE

Preparation Directions:

1. Introduce this game by leading a class discussion focused on the four basic food groups.

2. Cut pictures of food from magazines (or draw pictures) and paste on index cards. Prepare twenty to thirty cards.

3. Provide a chalkboard, chalk, and erasers.

Player Directions:

1. This game is for any number of players. Players are divided into two equal teams.

2. The food cards are shuffled and placed near the chalkboard.

3. One student or the teacher draws a card and shows it to the first player on each team.

4. At a given signal, the players write the name of the food on the chalkboard.

5. The first player to spell the word correctly wins one point.

6. If the player can tell in which basic food group the food belongs, another point is awarded.

7. The game continues until one team scores twenty points and wins the game.

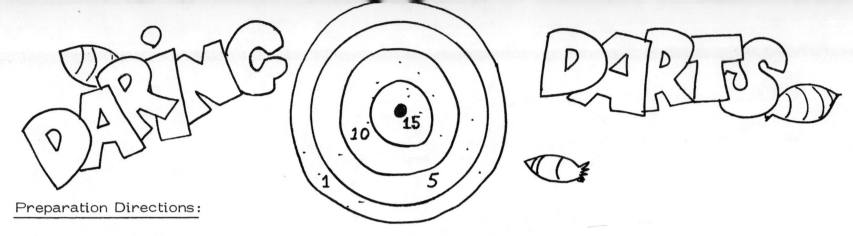

Preparation Directions:

1. Use a black felt tip marker and heavy drawing paper to make a target. Attach the target to a cork bulletin board.

2. Use small pieces of wood and nails to make darts.

3. Cover four small boxes with gift wrapping paper or contact paper.

4. Write the number 1 on a box. Write the number 5 on a box. Write the number 10 on a box. Write the number 15 on a box.

5. Print different spelling words on twenty-four small squares of tagboard. The spelling words should be on four levels of difficulty.

6. The less difficult words are placed in Box 1. Words at the next level of difficulty are placed in Box 5. Words at the next level are placed in Box 10, and the most difficult words are placed in Box 15.

Player Directions:

1. This game is for two, three, or four players.

2. The first player throws a dart at the target. If the dart lands on 5, one of the players draws a card from Box 5 and pronounces the word. If the player who threw the dart can spell the word, he or she receives five points.

3. If the dart lands on 15, a word from Box 15 is drawn, etc.

4. The game continues until one player scores thirty points and wins the game.

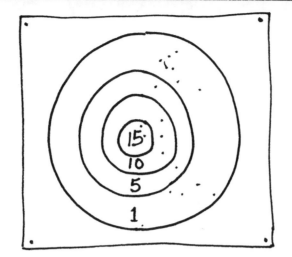

Dazzling Detectives

Preparation Directions:

1. Use tagboard to make thirty magnifying glasses. The magnifying glasses on the following page can be used as patterns.

2. Write a word from the monthly spelling list on the underside of each magnifying glass.

3. Write a clue about the word on the top of each magnifying glass.

4. Provide a kitchen timer.

5. Provide writing paper and pencils.

Player Directions:

1. This game is for two, three, or four players.

2. The magnifying glasses are arranged on a table to enable the students to see and read the word clues.

3. Each student has a piece of writing paper and a pencil.

4. The kitchen timer is set for ten minutes.

5. At a given signal, each player reads a word clue and writes the word on the writing paper.

6. The game continues until the timer stops.

7. The players look on the underside of the magnifying glasses to check the correct spelling of the words. The player with the most words spelled correctly wins the game.

Preparation Directions:

1. Mount the game board on poster board.

2. Provide a marker for each player.

3. Print the following words on small squares of poster board.

cut	sit	hit	mop	shine	plan	hop
have	bat	live	love	top	drive	spin
swim	fan	come	grin	stroke	bake	run

Player Directions:

1. This game is for two players.

2. Each player selects a marker.

3. The cards are shuffled and placed face down on the game board.

4. The first player draws a card and reads the word. The player must add <u>ing</u> to the word by doubling the last letter and adding <u>ing</u>, or must drop the last letter before adding <u>ing</u>. If the player is correct, he moves forward one space.

5. The game continues until one player reaches "Finish" and wins the game.

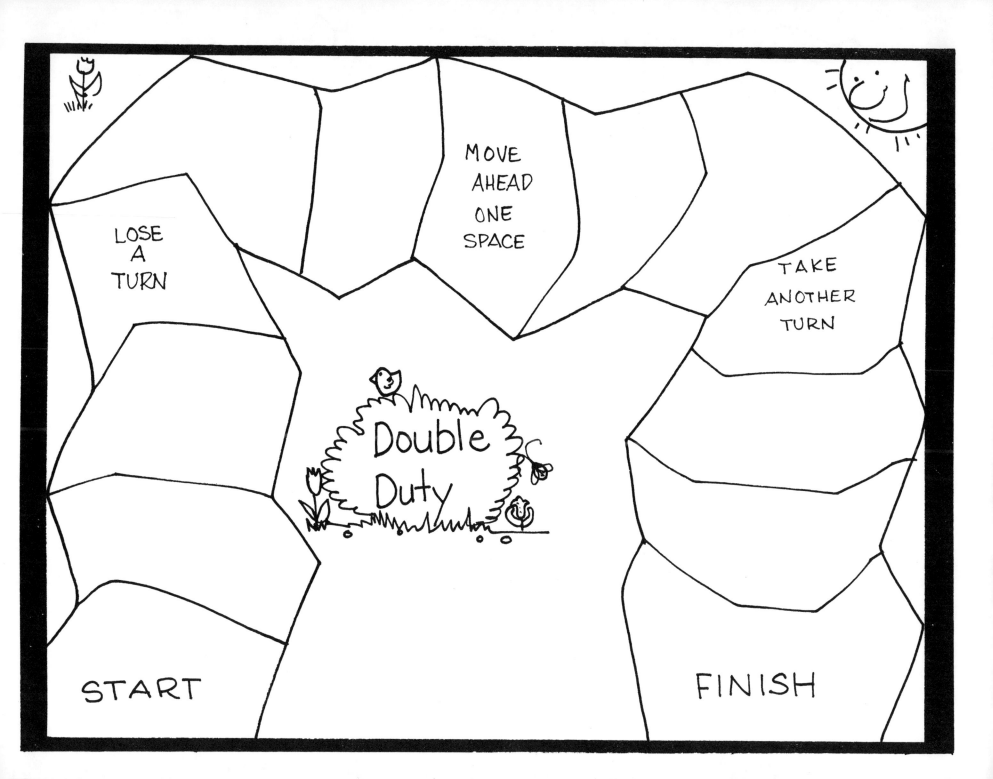

Preparation Directions:

1. Cut a gallon plastic milk container in half.

2. Cover the milk container with aluminum foil to resemble a crystal ball. Leave an opening at the top of the crystal ball.

3. Print the following words on small squares of tagboard:

grow	do	swim	play	drink	eat	write	dig
grew	did	swam	played	drank	ate	wrote	dug

   Add other words that have present or past tense.

4. If the word is present tense write "past" on the tagboard square. If the word is past tense write "present" on the tagboard square.

5. Place words in the crystal ball.

Player Directions:

1. This game is for two, three, or four players.

2. One player is the fortune teller and draws five cards from the crystal ball. The fortune teller must try to spell the correct tense of the word on each card. If the word is spelled correctly, the fortune teller can keep the card. If the word is not spelled correctly, the card is placed back into the crystal ball.

3. The game continues until all the players have been the fortune teller.

4. The player with the most cards wins the game.

Funny Feelings

Preparation Directions:

Tape the following activity:

"Step right up, folks! The Feelings' Fun House is the most exciting show at the fair. The only admission is writing paper, pencils, and crayons. The next performance will begin immediately.

"As you enter the Feelings' Fun House you will see pictures on the walls, ceiling, and floor. Each picture portrays an emotion. Under each picture is a caption that gives a clue to the emotion that is displayed. Take a few minutes to look around the Feelings' Fun House, and then number your writing paper from one to fifteen.

"I will read the caption under each picture and you will write the emotion that you think the picture displays. Try to spell each emotion correctly.

1. It is dark and Johnny has not come home from school. Johnny's mother is looking for him. She is _____ (anxious).
2. Susan's mother and father are kissing. The emotion is _____ (love).
3. A ferocious dog is chasing the boy on a bike. The boy feels _____ (frightened).
4. Dewey is planning a camping trip but suddenly gets sick and cannot go. The emotion is _____ (disappointment).
5. Cathy has a new baby sister. Cathy will not get all the attention at home. At first she feels _____ (jealous) but soon she loves the baby very much.
6. The teacher is announcing that there will be no homework for two days. The students are displaying _____ (happiness).
7. Joe breaks Steve's new toy. Steve becomes very _____ (angry).
8. Snorky, the pet dog, dies and the family feels very _____ (sad).
9. Allen has a knot in his shoe lace. After trying for thirty minutes to loosen the knot, he becomes _____ (frustrated).

10. Daddy comes from work, sits down to read the newspaper, and falls asleep. He is _____ (tired).
11. Mrs. Davis lives all alone. At times she feels _____ (lonely).
12. The teacher is asking Patty a question, and she doesn't know the answer. Patty's face becomes red and she feels warm. She feels _____ (embarrassed).
13. Lisa tells a secret to Mary. Lisa knows Mary will not tell anyone the secret. Lisa _____ (trusts) Mary.
14. Fred was supposed to do his chores but he went to a movie. He feels _____ (guilty) about not doing the chores.
15. Jack slams the door on his finger. He feels _____ (pain).

"This is the end of the show at the Feelings' Fun House. As you leave, please check your answers. The answer key is posted on the door."

Provide an answer key.

Activity Directions:

1. Instruct students to listen to the tape and follow the directions.

2. Provide time for students to illustrate and discuss various feelings.

Preparation Directions:

1. Duplicate the pictures on the following page, draw pictures of various objects, or cut pictures from magazines of objects for students to spell.

2. Provide masking tape.

Player Directions:

1. This game is for any number of players.

2. Tape a picture on the back of each player, but do not let the player see the picture.

3. One player will give three clues about the picture on the other player's back. If the player can guess the name of the picture and spell the word correctly, the picture can be removed.

4. The game continues until all the pictures have been identified and spelled correctly.

Preparation Directions:

1. Mount the Holiday Hunt game board on colored poster board.

2. Ask the students to use tagboard to make a marker for the game. A symbol used for a holiday could be used as the theme for the marker.

3. Use poster board and a brass fastener to make a spinner.

Player Directions:

1. This game is for any number of players.

2. Each player places a marker on "Start".

3. The first player flips the spinner and moves the number of spaces shown.

4. The player must spell the holiday that the picture represents on the space.

5. If the holiday is misspelled, the player loses one turn.

6. If the month of the holiday can be spelled correctly, the player gets another turn.

7. The game continues until one player reaches "Finish" and wins the game.

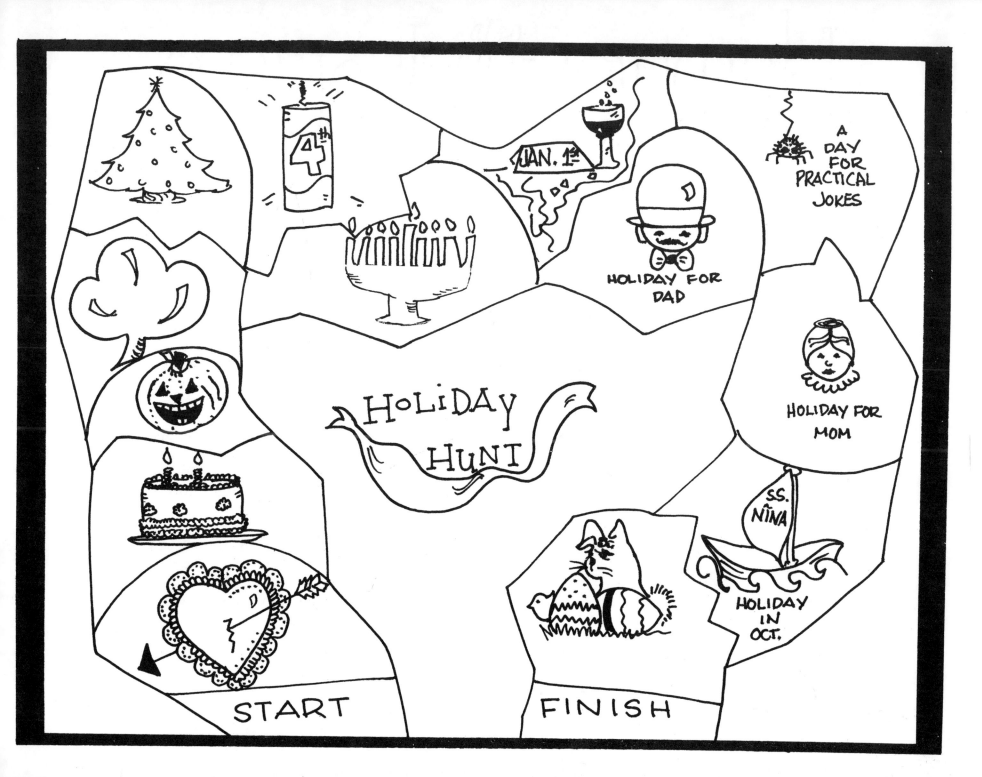

Homonym House

Preparation Directions:

Tape the following directions:

"You have been asked to design a house. However, this house is to be different, and no one has ever built one like it before. It is a homonym house because its occupants are homonyms. Since you are the architect, the homonym house can be any shape and can contain as many rooms as you wish. One building code that must be followed states that the homonym house must cover the lot, which is the piece of drawing paper. Turn the tape off, take a piece of drawing paper, and design your homonym house. Do not include furniture because this house contains homonyms. When the house is completed, turn the tape on for the next directions.

"Homonyms are words that sound alike, are spelled differently, and have different meanings. Listen to the sentences that contain homonyms and write the words in the house. You can write the homonyms anywhere in the house, but be sure you number each word so you can check the spelling of the words. See how cleverly you can fill the homonym house! (Allow enough time for students to write each homonym.)

1. My favorite flower is a rose. (flower)
2. The recipe has two cups of flour. (flour)
3. Mary threw the football. (threw)
4. The dog walked through the school. (through)
5. He has four apples. (four)
6. I bought a gift for my birthday. (for)
7. The horse's reins were leather. (reins)
8. When it rains, I play inside. (rains)
9. We ate cookies after class. (ate)
10. There are eight candles on the cake. (eight)
11. The sun was shining in my eyes. (sun)
12. My sister has one son. (son)
13. The road was covered with ice. (road)
14. I rode a horse on my vacation. (rode)
15. The boys made a snowman. (made)
16. The maid cleaned the motel room. (maid)
17. I would like to buy a toy. (would)
18. The fire needed more wood. (wood)
19. There was one piece of candy. (piece)
20. The countries signed a peace treaty. (peace)

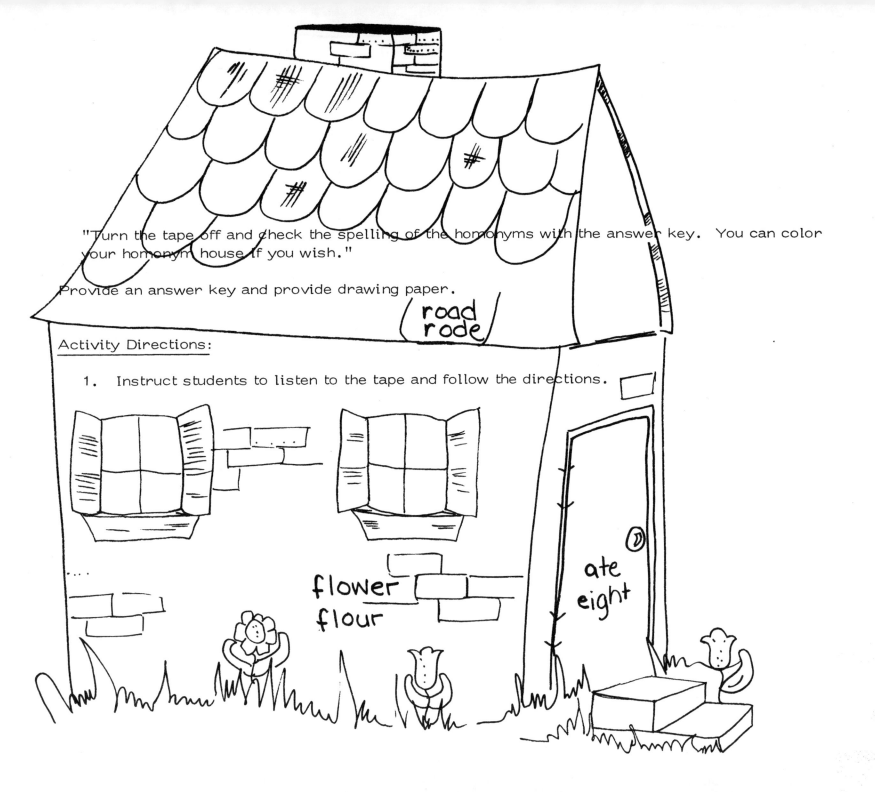

"Turn the tape off and check the spelling of the homonyms with the answer key. You can color your homonym house if you wish."

Provide an answer key and provide drawing paper.

Activity Directions:

1. Instruct students to listen to the tape and follow the directions.

HOPSCOTCH HOLDUP

Preparation Directions:

1. Use chalk to draw a large hopscotch pattern on the floor. If the classroom has carpet, outline a large hopscotch pattern with masking tape.

2. Place the following objects in the different hopscotch spaces.

clock	crayon
book	money (quarter, penny, nickel)
dictionary	magnet
ruler	glue
pencil	felt tip marker
paper	paper clip
eraser	scissors
globe	shoe

If these objects are not available, any object found in the classroom can be used.

3. Provide small stones to be used as markers.

Player Directions:

1. This game is for any number of players.

2. The first player tosses a marker in one of the hopscotch spaces. The player hops and picks up an object from the space in which the marker landed. After completing the hopscotch pattern, the player must spell the name of the object.

3. The player receives one point for each object spelled correctly.

4. The game continues until one player scores ten points and wins the game.

Preparation Directions:

1. Cut small pictures of various objects from a catalog.

2. Paste the pictures on small squares of tagboard.

Player Directions:

1. This game is for two or four players.

2. Each player needs paper and a pencil.

3. The picture cards are dealt and placed face down.

4. At a given signal, each player draws a picture card and writes the word for the picture.

5. The cards are drawn and the words written until all the cards have been used.

6. The first player to finish and spell all the words correctly wins the game.

Preparation Directions:

1. Provide a copy of the map and crayons for each student.

Player Directions:

1. This game is for two, three, or four players.

2. The first player points to an object on the map and asks another player to spell the word.

3. If the word is spelled correctly, the player who spelled the word can color the object on the map.

4. The players continue taking turns until one player has colored all the objects on the map.

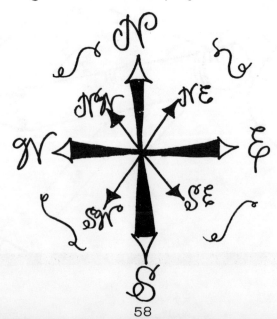

MATH MONSTER

Preparation Directions:

1. Mount the game board on heavy cardboard. Cover the game board with red cellophane.

2. Provide markers for each player.

3. Write addition, subtraction, multiplication, and division problems on forty index cards.

4. Provide paper for students' use.

Player Directions:

1. This game is for two, three, or four players.

2. Each player places a marker on "Start".

3. The math cards are shuffled and placed face down.

4. The first player draws a card and solves the math problem. The player must correctly spell the answer to the problem and the process used.

   Example: 16
            + 15
            ----
             31   —   Player spells the words t-h-i-r-t-y o-n-e and a-d-d-i-t-i-o-n

5. If the words are spelled correctly, the player moves one space on the game board.

6. The game continues until one player reaches the "Math Monster" and wins the game.

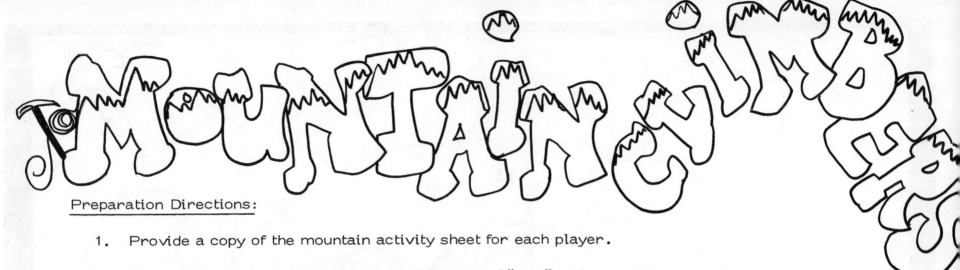

Mountain Climbers

Preparation Directions:

1. Provide a copy of the mountain activity sheet for each player.

2. Cut an old sheet or scraps of fabric into thirty 2" x 6" strips.

3. Use a felt tip marker to print a variety of spelling words on the strips of fabric. The words can be from a monthly or six weeks' spelling list, and should include several levels of difficulty.

4. Provide two six-foot ropes.

5. Attach the words to the rope with the most difficult words at the top of the rope.

6. Hang the ropes in the doorway of the classroom.

Player Directions:

1. This game is for two players.

2. Each player has a mountain activity sheet, and each player selects a word rope.

3. The first player pronounces the first word on the rope. The second player starts climbing the mountain by writing the word on the mountain activity sheet.

4. The game continues until all the words have been spelled correctly.

5. The first player to reach the top of the mountain wins the game.

Park and Lock

Preparation Directions:

1. Provide a copy of the parking lot for each student.

2. Provide crayons for students to draw cars, trucks, or motorcycles in the parking lot.

3. Write a variety of words for students to spell on thirty index cards. The weekly spelling list or words related to a specific topic of interest may be used.

Player Directions:

1. This game is for two students.

2. The word cards are shuffled and dealt to the players.

3. The first player draws a word card and pronounces the word to the second player. The second player spells the word.

4. If the word is correctly spelled, the second player can draw and color a car, truck, or motorcycle in a parking space.

5. The game continues until all the words have been spelled. The player who has the most cars, trucks, or motorcycles in the parking lot wins the game.

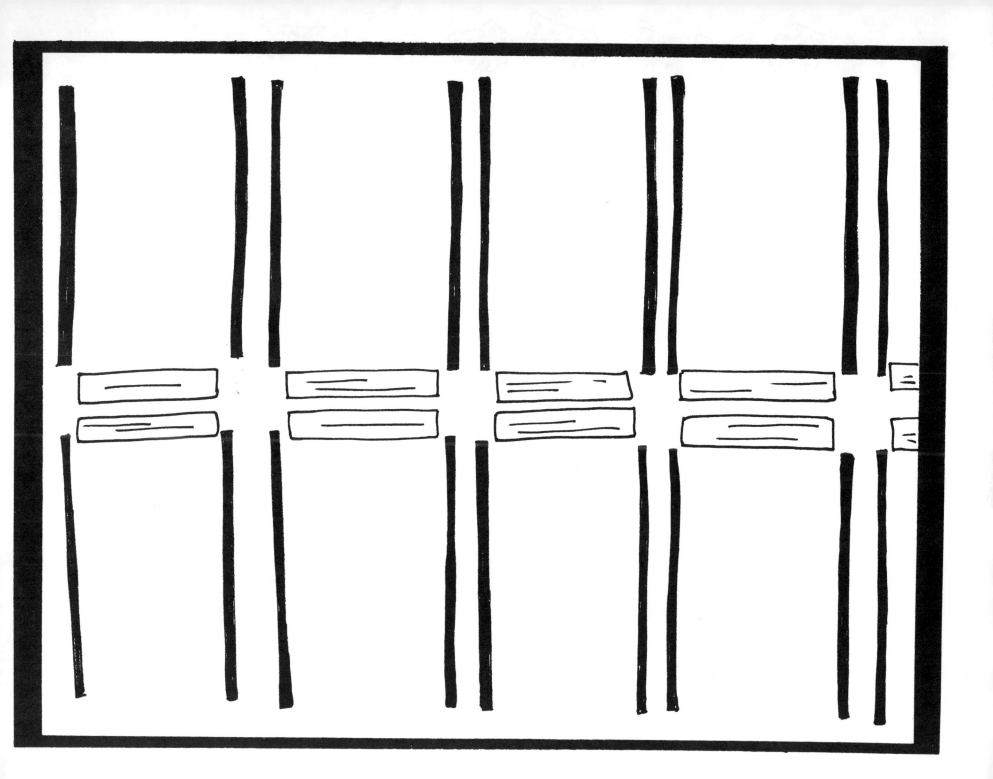

PERFECT ENDING

Preparation Directions:

1. Cut enough 4" x 6" cards from tagboard for each player to have a card. Use a permanent felt tip marker to divide the cards into twenty squares (similar to Bingo cards). Print one letter on each card.

2. Cover a small box or potato chip can with adhesive paper. Label the box "Perfect Ending". Fill the box with small pictures of one single item pasted on one-inch squares of pastel colored construction paper. The pictures may be cut from old workbooks, magazines, or drawn with colored felt tip pins.

3. Provide writing paper, pencils, and tokens such as beans or pebbles for each player.

Player Directions:

1. This game is for any number of players.

2. One child is elected "caller". All other players should have cards, tokens, writing paper, and pencils.

3. The "caller" draws one picture from the box and pronounces it. All other players look on their card for the last letter of the word called. If the letter is found a token is placed in the square and the word is written on the writing paper.

4. The first player to cover a complete row (Bingo style) calls "Perfect Ending".

5. The caller checks the words and if they are spelled correctly the player wins the game and becomes the next caller.

PERFECT ENDING!

d	h	y	s
r	n	i	t
e	g	f	k
x	p	c	b
z	m	w	o

Pick Pockets

Preparation Directions:

1. Color the clown with felt tip markers. Mount the colored clown on poster board. (A larger clown can be made with an overhead projector using the clown as a pattern.)

2. Cut slits in the clown's trousers to form pockets.

3. Write either <u>short</u>, <u>long</u>, <u>ar</u>, <u>or</u>, <u>er</u>, or <u>ir</u> on thirty strips of tagboard.

4. Place the strips in the clown's pockets.

Player Directions:

1. This game is for any number of players.

2. The group is divided into two teams.

3. The clown is placed on the chalkboard rack.

4. One player on the first team takes a strip from the clown's pockets. The player must spell a word that contains that sound.

5. If the word is spelled correctly, the team receives one point.

6. The game continues until the clown's pockets are empty.

7. The team with the most points wins the game.

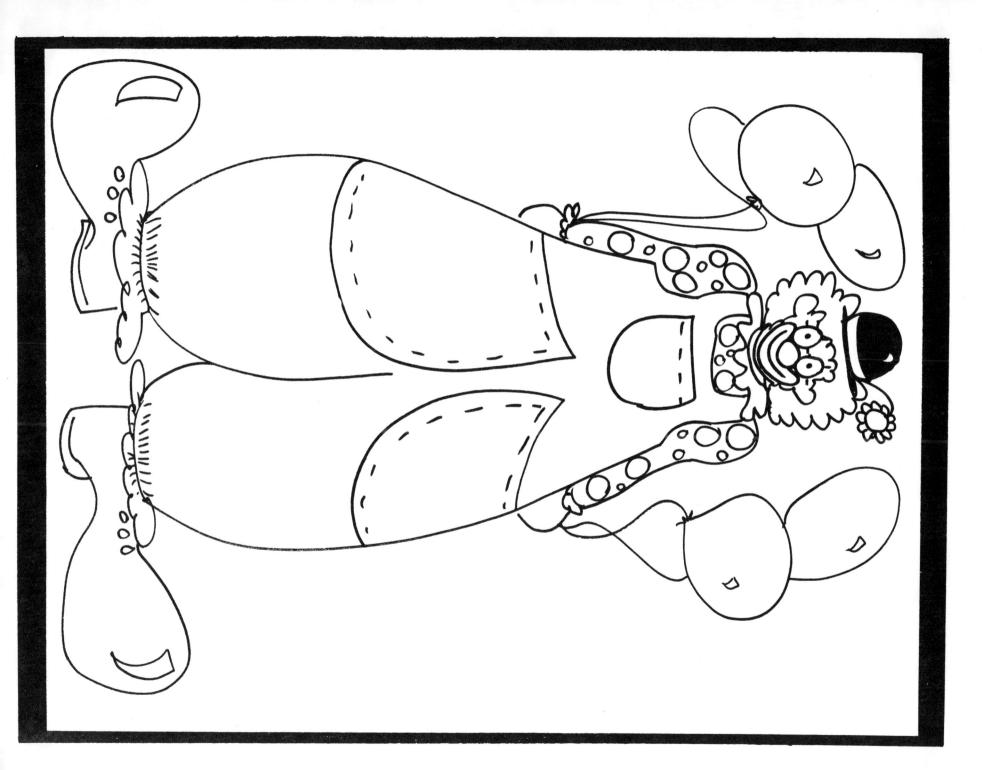

Picture Play

Preparation Directions:

1. To make the Picture Play game board more durable, it could be pasted on a piece of poster board and covered with clear contact paper.

2. Provide a marker for each player.

3. Provide a die.

Player Directions:

1. This game is for two, three, or four players.

2. Each player places a marker on "Start".

3. The first player throws the die and moves the correct number of spaces.

4. The player must spell a word that relates to the picture and the word on the space.

   Example: If the player lands on "flower", a name for a kind of flower must be spelled.

5. If the word is spelled correctly, the player can keep the marker on the space.

6. If the word is misspelled, the player must go back two spaces.

7. The game continues until one player reaches "Finish" and wins the game.

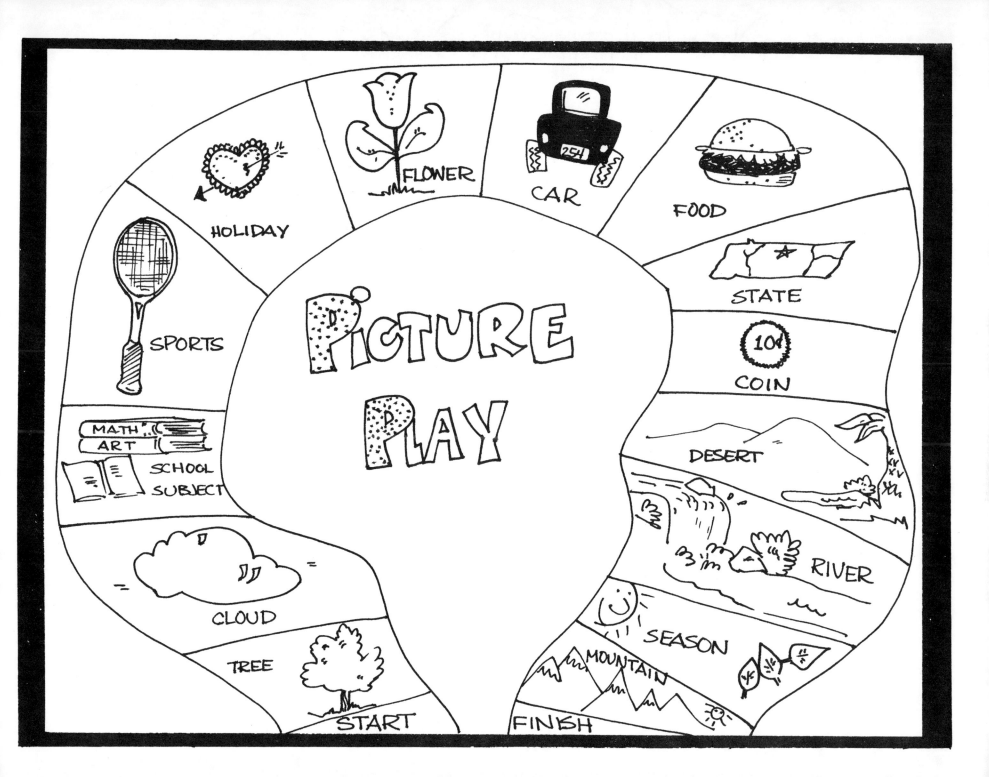

Plural Picnic

Preparation Directions:

1. Use mural or brown paper to cut a three-foot square to be used as a tablecloth.

2. Cut pictures illustrating one specific object from magazines, and paste the pictures on the paper tablecloth.

3. Provide a picnic basket or cover a shoe box with attractive paper.

4. Fold the paper tablecloth and place it inside the picnic basket or box.

5. Place two clipboards with writing paper and two pencils in the picnic basket or box.

6. A treat placed in the picnic basket for each player to enjoy after completing the game adds interest.

Player Directions:

1. This game is for two players.

2. Players may take the picnic basket to a quiet corner of the room, the hall, or outside.

3. The players spread the tablecloth and write the plural for each picture that is on the tablecloth.

4. When all the plural words have been written correctly, the players enjoy the picnic treat.

Preparation Directions:

1. Cut a picture from a magazine and paste it on a piece of cardboard.

2. Cut the picture into puzzle pieces.

3. Write the definition of a word on the back of each puzzle piece.

4. Place the puzzle pieces in a brightly covered box.

Player Directions:

1. This game is for two or three players.

2. The first player draws a puzzle piece, reads the definition, pronounces the word, and attempts to spell the word.

3. If the player spells the word correctly, the puzzle piece is placed on the table. If the word is not spelled correctly, the puzzle piece is placed back in the box.

4. The game continues until all the words have been spelled correctly and the puzzle has been completed.

RAIN DROP DELIGHT

Preparation Directions:

1. Hang a colorful umbrella upside down in a section of the classroom that allows for uninterrupted traffic flow.

2. Cut raindrops from heavy construction paper.

3. Use a permanent felt tip marker to draw pictures of words from center topics, content areas, or other topics of current interest on the raindrops. For variety, pictures might be cut from old workbooks or from magazines.

4. Use sewing thread or color-coordinated gift thread to hang raindrops from the umbrella so that they will be at a convenient height for the student to read.

5. Place paper and pencils near the umbrella. (Cushions and a comfortable rug would add a nice touch, too.)

6. Prepare an answer key and a score card and place them near the umbrella.

Player Directions:

1. The whole class can participate in this activity.

2. During "free time" students may go to the umbrella, turn it slowly, and try to spell correctly as many words as possible.

3. The words are written and checked for accuracy according to the answer key.

4. Upon completion of the self-check, the student is free to add his name to the score card and to record his score. (This step should be entirely optional and not a requirement.)

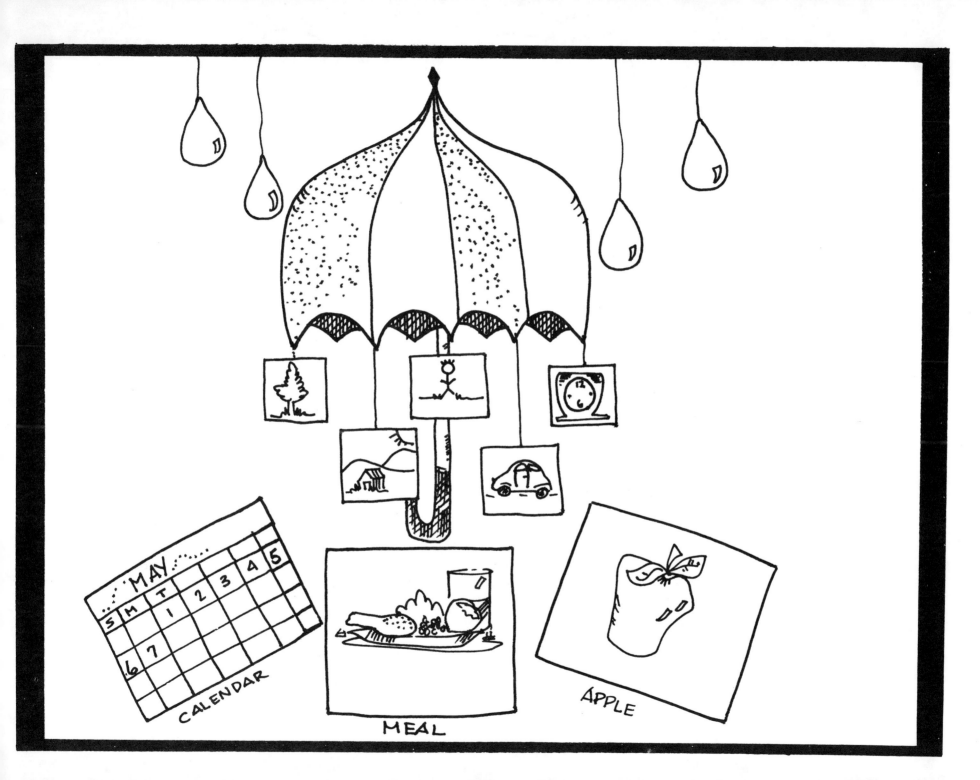

RIGHT OR WRONG

Preparation Directions:

1. Mount the game board on poster board. Cover the game board with clear contact paper or laminate the game board.

2. Provide markers for each player.

3. Write a variety of spelling words, unit words, or words from a spelling list on twenty index cards.

4. Write incorrectly spelled words from the same list on twenty index cards.

Player Directions:

1. This game is for two, three, or four players.

2. The markers are placed on the game board. The cards are shuffled and placed on the game board.

3. The first player draws a card. The player must decide whether or not the word is spelled correctly. If the word is not spelled correctly, the player must spell it correctly.

4. The player moves one space on the game board for each correct answer.

5. The game continues until one player reaches "finish" and wins the game.

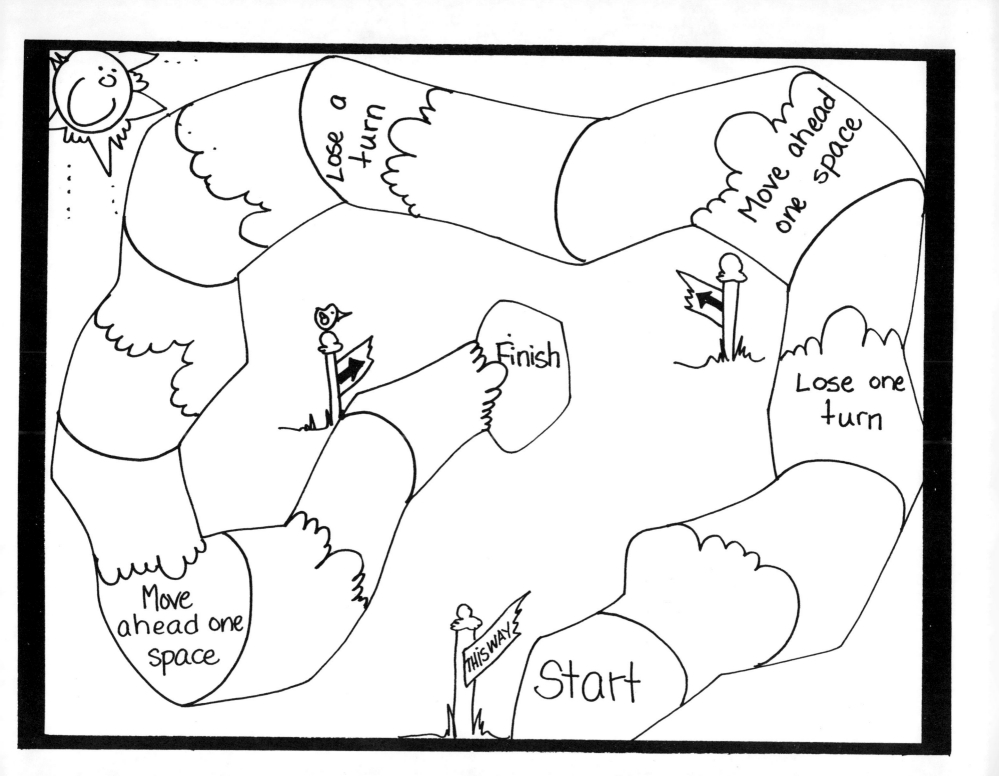

Role Review

Preparation Directions:

1. Write the following occupations on index cards:

doctor	plumber	minister	sanitation worker	pharmacist
dentist	electrician	chemist	dancer	bus driver
veterinarian	actress	salesman	teacher	nurse
lawyer	author	policeman	artist	pilot
		football coach		

   Other occupations can be added to this list so that each student will have an occupation card.

2. Cover a shoe box with brightly colored paper, and place the occupation cards inside the shoe box.

3. Provide drawing paper, crayons, pencils, and writing paper.

4. Duplicate the activity sheet.

Activity Directions:

1. This activity can be used with the entire class.

2. Each student draws an occupation card from the shoe box.

3. Ask the students to use a piece of drawing paper to draw clues relating to the occupation to enable the other students to guess the occupation more easily.

4. The first student pantomimes the occupation and the other students spell the occupation on writing paper.

5. The activity continues until all the occupations have been pantomimed and spelled correctly.

Preparation Directions:

1. Print words that have a prefix, suffix, or ending added on forty index cards.

    Example: thankful   repaint   adding

2. Provide a chalkboard, chalk, erasers, and a small bell.

Player Directions:

1. This game is for any number of players.

2. The group is divided into two equal teams.

3. The word cards are shuffled.

4. One student or the teacher draws a card, reads the word, and taps the bell.

5. One student from each group hops to the board and writes the root word and either the prefix, suffix, or ending.

6. The first person to spell correctly the root word and prefix, suffix, or ending wins a point for the team.

7. The game continues until one team scores twenty points and wins the game.

Shake and Make

Preparation Directions:

1. Forty wooden cubes are needed for this game. The cubes should be one inch square and can be secured from a lumber company. If wooden cubes are not available, squares of heavy cardboard can be substituted.

2. Use a red permanent felt tip marker to print different letters on twenty of the cubes. Use a blue permanent felt tip marker to print different letters on twenty of the cubes.

3. Cover two large jars with brightly colored contact or tissue paper.

4. Provide a kitchen timer.

Player Directions:

1. This game is for two players.

2. Twenty cubes are placed in each covered jar. The kitchen timer is set for three minutes.

3. The object of the game is for the players to try to make as many words as possible within the three-minute time period.

4. The players shake the containers and spill the letters.

5. Words that are made with red letters count five points. Words that are made with blue letters count three points.

6. The remaining letters are placed in the containers and the game continues until one player has twenty points and wins the game.

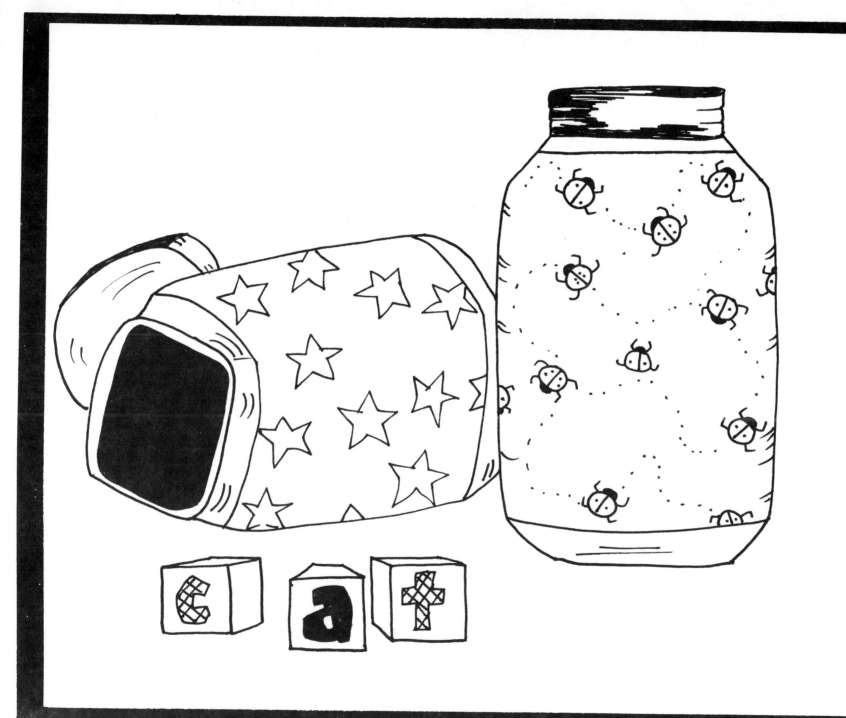

Sight Seeing

Preparation Directions:

1. Provide a copy of the bus for each student.

2. Cut slits in the bus to enable students to place the word cards inside.

3. Write the following words on strips of tagboard.

museum	park	bridge	factory
university	building	garden	zoo
hospital	ocean	mountain	airport
church	ship	statue	river

The monthly spelling word list may be used.

Player Directions:

1. This game is for any number of players.

2. Each player has a copy of the bus.

3. The word cards are shuffled and placed face down.

4. The first player draws a word card, pronounces the word, and asks another player to spell the word.

5. The player who spelled the word correctly can place the card in the bus.

6. The game continues until all the words have been spelled correctly.

7. The player who has the most cards in the bus wins the game.

Silent Scoop

Preparation Directions:

Tape the following directions. After each asterisk pronounce the word again, tap a bell, and allow enough time for students to write the word.

"There was once a knight* who lived in a castle* all alone. Everyone thought* the castle was haunted so the knight decided to have a party to prove that the castle was not haunted.

"The party began at seven o'clock with a sound of a loud whistle*. The guests* were startled and thought a ghost* had made the sound. The mayor's daughter* fainted but the other folks* only sighed*. Everyone was having a good time dancing and playing games until a crash came from one of the rooms.

"This castle must be haunted," exclaimed one man.

"But after investigating, the crash was found to be only dishes that had fallen from the cupboard*. After two hours*, the guests were invited to tour the castle. Each person climbed* the stairs to the second floor. Suddenly everyone stopped to listen* to a scream*. A lady had cut her thumb* on the knight's armor.

"A rope with several knots* hung from the hall ceiling*. The knight explained that the rope was the holder for a potted plant. Of course the guests had guessed* the rope was responsible for someone's death. A strange picture was displayed on an easel* near the fireplace. As the guests stood gazing at the picture, a secret door suddenly opened. The frightened* guests ran through* the door that led downstairs. How relieved they were to be back in the party room again! At last the guests knew* that the castle was not haunted.

"The party continued with laughter and merriment. At midnight* the guests bade good night to the knight and went home happy to know that the house was not haunted."

Provide an answer key showing the correct spelling and the silent letters of each word.

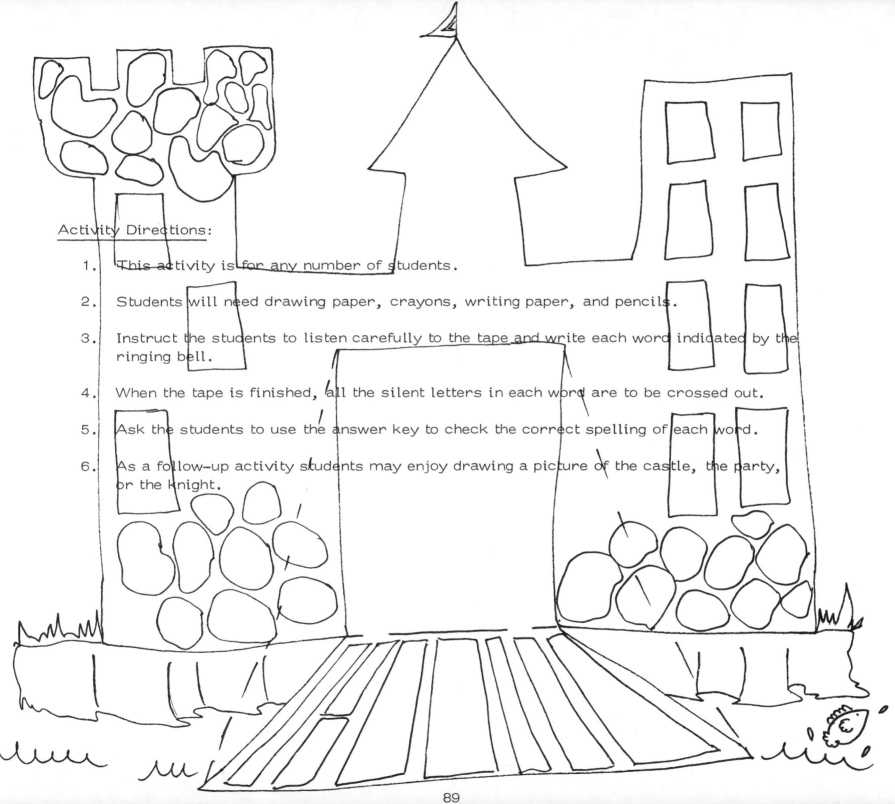

Activity Directions:

1. This activity is for any number of students.

2. Students will need drawing paper, crayons, writing paper, and pencils.

3. Instruct the students to listen carefully to the tape and write each word indicated by the ringing bell.

4. When the tape is finished, all the silent letters in each word are to be crossed out.

5. Ask the students to use the answer key to check the correct spelling of each word.

6. As a follow-up activity students may enjoy drawing a picture of the castle, the party, or the knight.

Preparation Directions:

1. Make the game board shown on the following page on a large sheet of plastic or mural paper.

2. Provide a bean bag.

Player Directions:

1. This game is for two, three, or four players.

2. Place the game board on the floor.

3. Standing three feet from the game board, the first player throws the bean bag.

4. If the bean bag lands on the space marked "noun", the player must spell a word that is a noun, etc.

5. If the word is spelled correctly, the player receives one point.

6. The game continues until one player receives ten points and wins the game.

Spelling Scramble

Preparation Directions:

1. Write the weekly spelling words on strips of tagboard.

2. Cut the words so that each letter is separate.

3. Place the letters of each word in an envelope.

4. Place the envelopes in an attractively covered shoe box.

Player Directions:

1. This game is for two players.

2. Each player selects an envelope from the box.

3. At a given signal, the players try to unscramble the spelling words.

4. The first player to spell the word correctly receives one point.

5. The game continues until all the words have been spelled.

6. The player that receives the most points wins the game.

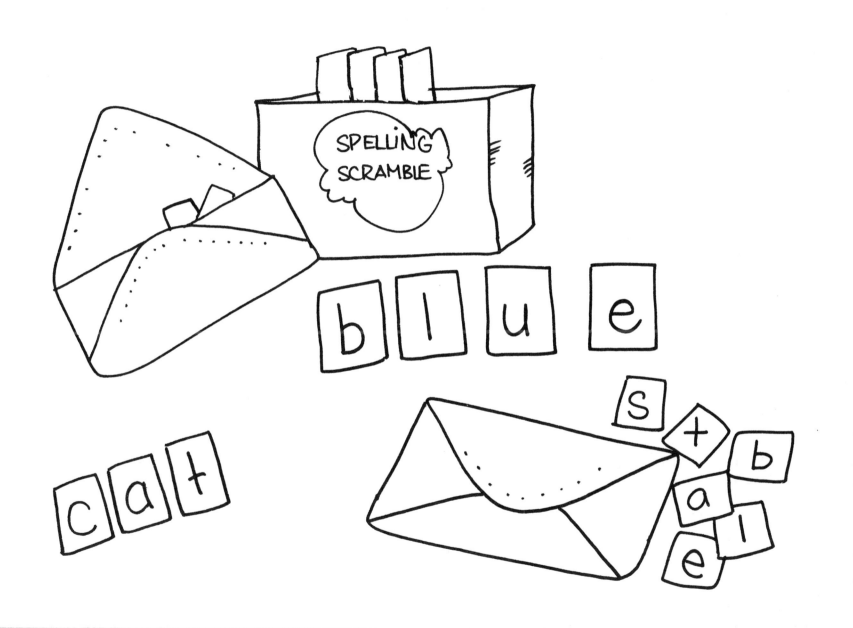

SPINNER SPREE

Preparation Directions:

1. Use a piece of plastic or heavy brown paper to make a large circle.

2. Draw different pictures around the outside edge of the circle. The pictures can be related to a particular unit of study, a holiday, or other special topic.

3. Provide a soft drink bottle.

Player Directions:

1. This game is for any number of players.

2. The circle is placed on the floor.

3. The players sit behind the pictures.

4. One player sits in the middle and spins the bottle.

5. When the bottle stops spinning and points to a picture, the player nearest the picture must spell the word.

6. If the word is correctly spelled, the player swaps places with the bottle spinner.

7. The game continues until all the words have been spelled.

STAR GAZERS

Preparation Directions:

1. Cut twenty stars of different sizes from yellow construction paper.

2. Write a word on each star that can be easily matched to a rhyming word.

3. Use string to hang the stars from the ceiling or tape them to the underside of a table.

4. Make a large star for each player. Draw twenty lines on each star.

5. Provide an answer key.

Player Directions:

1. This game is for any number of players and can be used as a free-choice activity.

2. The players gaze at the stars and think of a rhyming word for each star. The rhyming words are written on the lines on the large star.

3. Players use the answer key to check the spelling of the rhyming words.

Surprise Store

Preparation Directions:

Tape the following directions:

"Welcome to the most unusual and exciting store in the world. As you enter the front door, you see all the items for sale...except these items are really unusual. Everything that can be purchased is attractively wrapped in packages of all sizes. The customers do not know what is inside the packages. The only identification on each package is a number. You are invited to shop today in this "Surprise Store". There are many packages, but if you can correctly identify ten of the packages, you can select any five to keep as your very own.

"Before you begin shopping take a sheet of paper, a pencil, and crayons. Number your paper from one to ten. Listen carefully to all the clues in order to identify each package. When you are sure you know the name of the object in the package, write it beside the correct number. Good luck!

"Package 1: This object can be used to wake you up in the mornings. You can also learn about the weather, news, or listen to music with it. It is a _____.

"Package 2: This package is long. The object is very useful, especially if it rains. Some people use it to protect themselves from the sun. It is an _____.

"Package 3: There are two objects in this package. You sometimes use them inside, but other times they may be used outside. They look like boots, but each one has four wheels. They are _____.

"Package 4: This object can contain different kinds of information. It is often used for school work and many times just for pleasure. You must be able to read to use it. It is a _____.

"Package 5: This package weighs one pound and has a fancy wrap. It tastes good and is a popular gift item for young and old. It is _____.

"Package 6: This object can be different sizes, lengths, colors, and shapes. It is worn around the neck for decoration. It is a _____.

"Package 7: This package would be fun to have in the summer. You need milk, eggs, sugar, ice, and salt to use it. After turning it by hand or using electricity, the ingredients become hard. It is an _____.

"Package 8: These are used to keep you warm. One is worn around the neck and the others keep your hands warm, but have no fingers. This package contains a _____ and _____.

"Package 9: This object is round and very flat. You need a machine to listen to it. It comes in different speeds and different themes. It is a _____.

"Package 10: This object can be used as a means of transportation or for fun. It has two wheels and people of all ages ride it. It is a _____.

"I hope you've had fun shopping. Now let's check to see if you identified all the packages by correctly spelling each object.

1. radio   3. roller skates   5. candy   7. ice cream freezer   9. record
2. umbrella   4. book   6. necklace   8. scarf (or muffler) and mittens 10. bicycle

"If you spelled correctly the name of each object, draw pictures of each of the five objects you selected to keep for your very own."

Activity Directions:

1. This activity is for any number of students.

2. Students will need drawing paper, crayons, writing paper, and pencils.

3. Instruct students to listen to the tape and follow the directions.

4. Provide time for students to share the completed pictures.

Preparation Directions:

1. Print "Beginning" on ten squares of tagboard, print "Middle" on ten squares of tagboard, and print "End" on ten squares of tagboard.

2. Provide three tea cups or three paper cups.

3. Cut writing paper in strips for students to use to write words.

4. Provide a jar of instant tea.

Player Directions:

1. This game is for three players.

2. Each player selects a tea cup or paper cup, and takes ten strips of writing paper.

3. The tagboard squares are shuffled and placed face down.

4. The first player draws a card and shows it to the other players. If the card has "Beginning" on it, the players must write a word beginning with "t". If the card has "Middle" on it, the players must write a word that has "t" in the middle of the word. If the card has "End" on it, the players must write a word that ends with "t".

5. The first player to write a word correctly places the strip of writing paper in the cup.

6. The players continue to play until all cards are drawn.

7. The player with the most words spelled correctly wins the game.

8. Players will enjoy a cup of instant tea!

Preparation Directions:

1. Cover three shoe boxes with gift wrapping paper.

2. Print a variety of spelling words on index cards. The words should have two levels of difficulty.

3. Place the words in the three shoe boxes.

4. Provide a table and three chairs.

Player Directions:

1. The entire class can participate in this activity.

2. This activity is presented as a television program.

3. One student acts as the Master of Ceremonies.

4. The "MC" asks for three volunteers from the audience.

5. The covered shoe boxes are placed on the table.

6. The first player selects a word from one of the boxes. Without looking at the word, the player hands it to the "MC".

7. The "MC" pronounces the word and the player must try to spell it.

8. If the word is spelled correctly, the player receives five points.

9. The game continues until one player has fifty points.

10. This activity can be repeated until all the students in the class have "starred" on television.

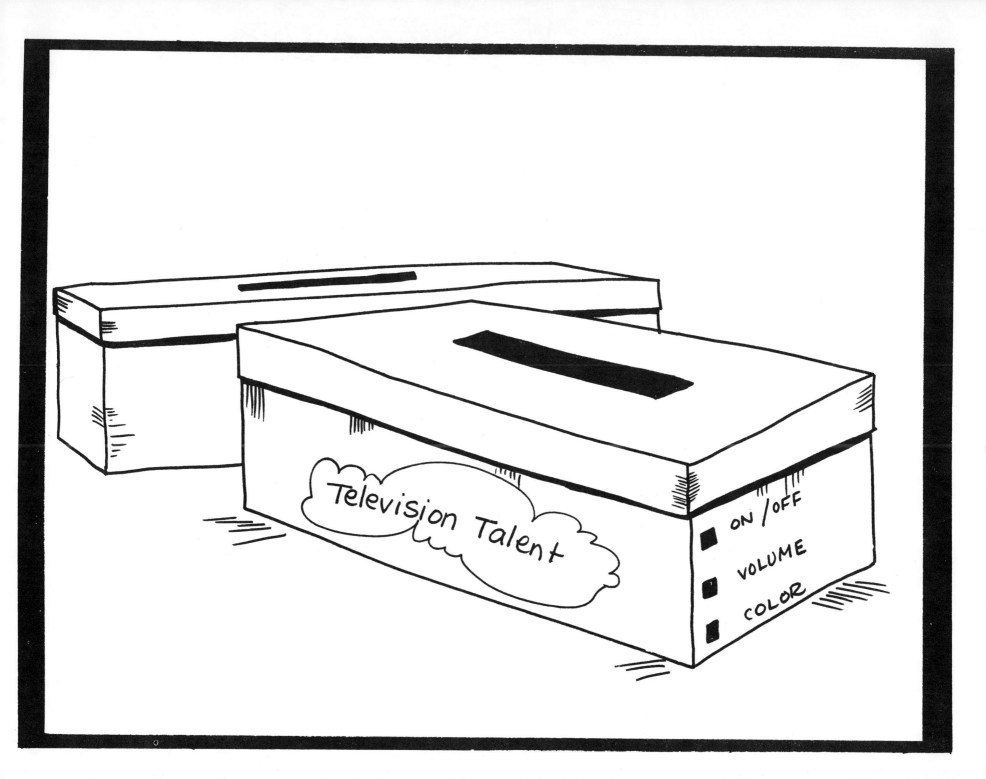

Travel Tips

<u>Preparation Directions:</u>

Tape the following directions:

"Congratulations! You have been selected to receive a free vacation of your choice. You will leave in one week so you need to make some plans for the trip. Take a sheet of writing paper and a pencil and listen carefully to the directions.

"Think about all the fun places you would like to go, and write the name of the vacation spot you will visit. In what state is it located? Write the name of the state. Now that you have decided where to go, you must pack your suitcase. Make a list of all the things that will be in your suitcase. You will need to telephone a travel agency to help you plan your trip. Write the name of the travel agency you will call. List the methods of transportation you could use to reach your destination. Now circle the kind of transportation that you will use. How long will it take you to reach your vacation spot? Write the number of hours or days you think you will need to travel. The travel agency will make the necessary reservations for your lodging. Where will you sleep each night? Write the name of the town. The travel agency will also give you brochures about interesting places to visit on your vacation. List the places you will plan to visit. Plan your recreation activities and write the names of all the fun things you hope to do. You will enjoy eating at the different restaurants. Make a list of the exciting foods you will eat. Don't forget snacks! You will surely want to send a picture postcard to a friend. Write the message you will write on the picture postcard. The last thing you will want to do on your trip is to buy a souvenir. Write the name of a souvenir you would like to buy.

"Now that your trip is all planned, take a sheet of drawing paper and draw a picture illustrating your vacation. Don't forget to include yourself in the picture!

"Share your finished picture with the class. The teacher will check the spelling words."

Activity Directions:

1. This activity is for any number of students.

2. Students will need drawing paper, crayons, writing paper, and pencils.

3. Instruct students to listen to the tape and follow the directions.

4. Provide time for students to share the completed pictures.

5. As a follow-up activity students may wish to write a story about a favorite vacation or about a vacation they would like to take.

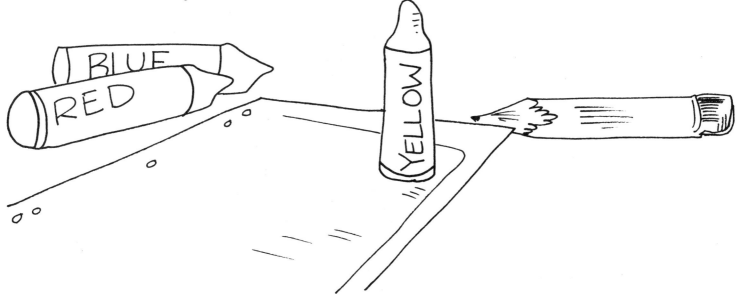

Preparation Directions:

1. Write antonyms, homonyms, and synonyms on small squares of tagboard.

2. Cover three coffee cans with contact paper.

3. Place the antonyms in one can; the homonyms in one can; and the synonyms in one can.

Player Directions:

1. This game is for two or four players.

2. The first player selects the antonym, homonym, or synonym can and draws a word card.

3. If an antonym card is drawn, the player must spell a word that could be an antonym for the word that was drawn, etc.

4. If the word is spelled correctly, the player receives one point.

5. The game continues until one player receives fifteen points and wins the game.

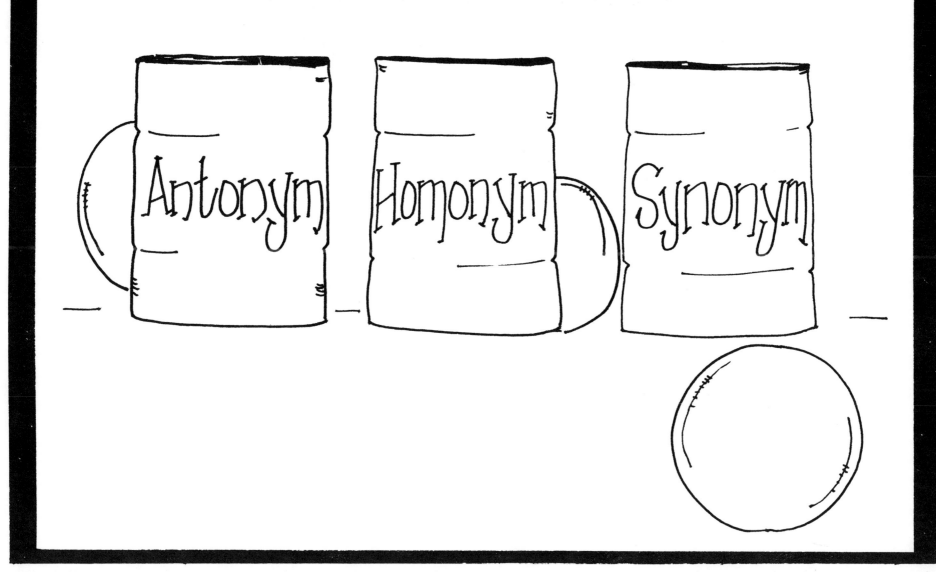

Preparation Directions:

1. Mount the game board on poster board. Cover the game board with blue cellophane.

2. Provide markers or ask the students to design markers.

3. Provide a die.

Player Directions:

1. This game is for two, three, or four players.

2. Each player places a marker on the "shell".

3. The first player rolls the die and moves the correct number of spaces.

4. If the space has "short a" on it, the player must spell a word containing a "short a" sound, etc.

5. If the space has "long a" on it, the player must spell a word containing a "long a" sound, etc.

6. If the player cannot spell the word correctly, the marker is moved back two spaces.

7. The game continues until one player reaches the "whale" and wins the game.

Window Shopping

Preparation Directions:

1. Draw a shopping center on a window shade or enlarge the picture on the following page.
   If a window shade is not available, a large piece of tagboard, plastic, or cloth can be used.

2. Cut holes in the shade to create the store windows.

3. Attach envelopes on the backs of the store windows so that students may reach inside them.

4. Print WHO on ten small squares of tagboard.
   Print WHAT on ten small squares of tagboard.
   Print WHERE on ten small squares of tagboard.
   Print WHEN on ten small squares of tagboard.

5. Place the tagboard squares inside the envelopes.

Player Directions:

1. This game is for any number of players.

2. The first player reaches inside a window and draws a card. If a "WHO" card is drawn, a word that answers "WHO" must be spelled, etc.

3. If the word is spelled correctly, the player keeps the card.

4. The game continues until there are no cards left inside the windows.

5. The player with the most cards wins the game.